"If anyone would come after Me, he must deny himself and take up his cross and follow Me. For whoever loses his life for Me will find it."

Matthew 16:24-25

The word of the LORD is right and true;
He is faithful in all He does.

Psalm 33:4

"You will call upon Me and come and pray to Me, and I will listen to you.
You will seek Me and find Me when you seek Me with all your heart."
Jeremiah 29:12-13

My soul finds rest in God alone; my salvation comes from Him.

Psalm 62:1

Delight yourself in the Lord
and He will give you the desires of your heart.
Psalm 37:4

The Lord is my light and my salvation – whom shall I fear?
The Lord is the stronghold of my life – of whom shall I be afraid?

Psalm 27:1

The Lord Himself goes before you and will be with you;
He will never leave you nor forsake you.

Deuteronomy 31:8

God is working in you, giving you the desire
to obey Him and the power to do what pleases Him.
Philippians 2:13

I can do everything through Him who gives me strength.
Philippians 4:13

If you want to know what God wants you to do –
ask Him, and He will gladly tell you.

James 1:5

Create in me a pure heart, O God,
and renew a steadfast spirit within me.
Psalm 51:10

If anyone is in Christ, he is a new creation;
the old has gone, the new has come!

2 Corinthians 5:17

Cast your cares on the Lord and He will sustain you.
Psalm 55:22

The Lᴏʀᴅ your God is with you, He is mighty to save.
He will take great delight in you, He will quiet you with His love.
Zephaniah 3:17

The LORD is faithful to all His promises and loving toward all He has made.

Psalm 145:13

In You, O Lord, do I put my trust and confidently take refuge;
let me never be put to shame or confusion!

Psalm 71:1

"Be strong and courageous. The Lᴏʀᴅ your God will be with you wherever you go."

Joshua 1:9

Depend on the Lord in whatever you do,
and your plans will succeed.
Proverbs 16:3

Since we have been justified through faith,
we have peace with God through our Lord Jesus Christ.

Romans 5:1

_____

_____

_____

_____

_____

_____

_____

_____

_____

_____

_____

_____

_____

_____

_____

_____

_____

_____

_____

The LORD is my rock, my fortress and my deliverer;
my God is my rock, in whom I take refuge.

Psalm 18:2

"If anyone would come after Me, he must deny himself and take up his cross and follow Me. For whoever loses his life for Me will find it."

Matthew 16:24-25

The word of the Lᴏʀᴅ is right and true;
He is faithful in all He does.
Psalm 33:4

The Lord is my strength, my shield from every danger.
I trust in Him with all my heart.

Psalm 28:7

In Him we have redemption through His blood,
the forgiveness of sins, in accordance with the riches of God's grace.

I trust in Your unfailing love. I will rejoice because You have rescued me.
I will sing to the Lord because He has been so good to me.

Psalm 13:5-6

Live a life of love, just as Christ loved us and gave Himself up for us as a fragrant offering and sacrifice to God.

Ephesians 5:2

"You will call upon Me and come and pray to Me, and I will listen to you.
You will seek Me and find Me when you seek Me with all your heart."
Jeremiah 29:12-13

My soul finds rest in God alone; my salvation comes from Him.

Psalm 62:1

Delight yourself in the LORD
and He will give you the desires of your heart.
Psalm 37:4

The Lord is my light and my salvation – whom shall I fear?
The Lord is the stronghold of my life – of whom shall I be afraid?

Psalm 27:1

The LORD Himself goes before you and will be with you;
He will never leave you nor forsake you.
Deuteronomy 31:8

God is working in you, giving you the desire
to obey Him and the power to do what pleases Him.

Philippians 2:13

I can do everything through Him who gives me strength.
Philippians 4:13

If you want to know what God wants you to do –
ask Him, and He will gladly tell you.

James 1:5

Create in me a pure heart, O God,
and renew a steadfast spirit within me.

Psalm 51:10

_____

_____

_____

_____

_____

_____

_____

_____

_____

_____

_____

_____

_____

_____

_____

_____

_____

_____

_____

_____

_____

If anyone is in Christ, he is a new creation;
the old has gone, the new has come!

2 Corinthians 5:17

Cast your cares on the Lord and He will sustain you.

Psalm 55:22

The LORD your God is with you, He is mighty to save.
He will take great delight in you, He will quiet you with His love.
Zephaniah 3:17

The Lord is faithful to all His promises and loving toward all He has made.

Psalm 145:13

In You, O Lord, do I put my trust and confidently take refuge;
let me never be put to shame or confusion!

Psalm 71:1

"Be strong and courageous. The Lord your God will be
with you wherever you go."
Joshua 1:9

Depend on the Lord in whatever you do,
and your plans will succeed.

Proverbs 16:3

Since we have been justified through faith,
we have peace with God through our Lord Jesus Christ.

Romans 5:1

The Lord is my rock, my fortress and my deliverer;
my God is my rock, in whom I take refuge.

Psalm 18:2

"If anyone would come after Me, he must deny himself and take up his cross and follow Me. For whoever loses his life for Me will find it."

Matthew 16:24-25

The word of the LORD is right and true;
He is faithful in all He does.

Psalm 33:4

The LORD is my strength, my shield from every danger.
I trust in Him with all my heart.

Psalm 28:7

In Him we have redemption through His blood,
the forgiveness of sins, in accordance with the riches of God's grace.

Ephesians 1:7

I trust in Your unfailing love. I will rejoice because You have rescued me.
I will sing to the Lord because He has been so good to me.

Psalm 13:5-6

Live a life of love, just as Christ loved us and gave Himself up for us as a fragrant offering and sacrifice to God.

Ephesians 5:2

"You will call upon Me and come and pray to Me, and I will listen to you.
You will seek Me and find Me when you seek Me with all your heart."

Jeremiah 29:12-13

My soul finds rest in God alone; my salvation comes from Him.

Psalm 62:1

Delight yourself in the LORD
and He will give you the desires of your heart.
Psalm 37:4

The Lord is my light and my salvation – whom shall I fear?
The Lord is the stronghold of my life – of whom shall I be afraid?
Psalm 27:1

The LORD Himself goes before you and will be with you;
He will never leave you nor forsake you.
Deuteronomy 31:8

God is working in you, giving you the desire
to obey Him and the power to do what pleases Him.
Philippians 2:13

I can do everything through Him who gives me strength.
Philippians 4:13

If you want to know what God wants you to do –
ask Him, and He will gladly tell you.

James 1:5

Create in me a pure heart, O God,
and renew a steadfast spirit within me.

Psalm 51:10

If anyone is in Christ, he is a new creation;
the old has gone, the new has come!

2 Corinthians 5:17

Cast your cares on the Lord and He will sustain you.
Psalm 55:22

The Lord your God is with you, He is mighty to save.
He will take great delight in you, He will quiet you with His love.

Zephaniah 3:17

The Lord is faithful to all His promises and loving toward all He has made.
Psalm 145:13

In You, O Lord, do I put my trust and confidently take refuge;
let me never be put to shame or confusion!

Psalm 71:1

"Be strong and courageous. The LORD your God will be
with you wherever you go."

Joshua 1:9

Depend on the Lord in whatever you do,
and your plans will succeed.
Proverbs 16:3

Since we have been justified through faith,
we have peace with God through our Lord Jesus Christ.

Romans 5:1

The LORD is my rock, my fortress and my deliverer;
my God is my rock, in whom I take refuge.
Psalm 18:2

"If anyone would come after Me, he must deny himself and take up his cross and follow Me. For whoever loses his life for Me will find it."

Matthew 16:24-25

The word of the LORD is right and true;
He is faithful in all He does.
Psalm 33:4

The Lord is my strength, my shield from every danger.
I trust in Him with all my heart.

Psalm 28:7

In Him we have redemption through His blood,
the forgiveness of sins, in accordance with the riches of God's grace.

Ephesians 1:7

I trust in Your unfailing love. I will rejoice because You have rescued me.
I will sing to the LORD because He has been so good to me.

Psalm 13:5-6

Live a life of love, just as Christ loved us and gave Himself up for us as a fragrant offering and sacrifice to God.

Ephesians 5:2

"You will call upon Me and come and pray to Me, and I will listen to you.
You will seek Me and find Me when you seek Me with all your heart."

Jeremiah 29:12-13

My soul finds rest in God alone; my salvation comes from Him.

Psalm 62:1

The LORD Himself goes before you and will be with you;
He will never leave you nor forsake you.

Deuteronomy 31:8

God is working in you, giving you the desire
to obey Him and the power to do what pleases Him.

Philippians 2:13

I can do everything through Him who gives me strength.
Philippians 4:13

If you want to know what God wants you to do –
ask Him, and He will gladly tell you.

James 1:5

Create in me a pure heart, O God,
and renew a steadfast spirit within me.

Psalm 51:10

If anyone is in Christ, he is a new creation;
the old has gone, the new has come!

2 Corinthians 5:17

Cast your cares on the LORD and He will sustain you.
Psalm 55:22

The Lᴏʀᴅ your God is with you, He is mighty to save.
He will take great delight in you, He will quiet you with His love.
Zephaniah 3:17

The LORD is faithful to all His promises and loving toward all He has made.

Psalm 145:13

In You, O Lord, do I put my trust and confidently take refuge;
let me never be put to shame or confusion!

Psalm 71:1

"Be strong and courageous. The LORD your God will be
with you wherever you go."

Joshua 1:9

Depend on the Lord in whatever you do,
and your plans will succeed.
Proverbs 16:3

Since we have been justified through faith,
we have peace with God through our Lord Jesus Christ.

The LORD is my rock, my fortress and my deliverer;
my God is my rock, in whom I take refuge.
Psalm 18:2

"If anyone would come after Me, he must deny himself and take up his cross and follow Me. For whoever loses his life for Me will find it."

Matthew 16:24-25

The word of the LORD is right and true;
He is faithful in all He does.

Psalm 33:4

The LORD is my strength, my shield from every danger.
I trust in Him with all my heart.

Psalm 28:7

In Him we have redemption through His blood,
the forgiveness of sins, in accordance with the riches of God's grace.

Ephesians 1:7

I trust in Your unfailing love. I will rejoice because You have rescued me.
I will sing to the LORD because He has been so good to me.

Psalm 13:5-6

Live a life of love, just as Christ loved us and gave Himself up for us as a
fragrant offering and sacrifice to God.

Ephesians 5:2